A Promise of Freedom:

The Declaration of Independence

By

Dr. Latina Campbell

Print ISBN: 978-1-966491-16-3

eBook ISBN: 978-1-966491-17-0

Printed in the United States of America

Story Corner Publishing & Consulting, Inc.

Chesapeake, VA 23321

Storycornerpublishing@yahoo.com

www.StoryCornerPublishing.com

Dedication

I dedicate this book to all the children who dream of becoming the
future president, members of Congress, judges, lawyers,
politicians, law enforcement, or even military.
Be fair and just with everyone and do everything in love and kindness.
Put God first and allow Him to lead you through every decision.

In the meantime, remember no matter who holds office
or what laws are passed, God has the final say and
remains in control. There's no need to worry about things
you see happen in the world, just pray to God. Prayer changes everything.

P.S.

I'm proud of you because you are brave!

Fun Facts

The Declaration of Independence is a foundational document of the United States, officially declaring the separation of the 13 American colonies from Great Britain. It was adopted by the Second Continental Congress on July 4, 1776, and outlines the reasons for this separation, including the assertion of inherent rights like life, liberty, and the pursuit of happiness.

Declaration of Independence:

This document, formally titled "The unanimous Declaration of the thirteen United States of America," proclaimed the colonies' independence from British rule.

Purpose:

The Declaration aimed to:

- Explain to the world why the colonies were separating from Great Britain.

- Establish the principles upon which the new nation would be founded

- **Key Points:**

  - **Natural Rights:** It asserts that all men are created equal and are endowed with unalienable rights, including the right to life, liberty, and the pursuit of happiness.

  - **Consent of the Governed:** Governments derive their just powers from the consent of the governed.

  - **Right to Revolution:** The people have the right to alter or abolish a government that becomes destructive of these ends.

  - **Grievances:** The Declaration includes a list of grievances against King George III and the British government, highlighting injustices that led to the colonists' decision to separate.

- **Significance:**

The Declaration of Independence has had a profound impact on the United States and on movements for independence and human rights worldwide. It is one of the most influential and widely circulated documents in history.

In 1776 · United States of America

3

A long time ago, across the sea,

The king made rules for you and me.

He lived in England, far away,

But told the colonies what to do each day.

The thirteen colonies tried to be heard,
But the king would not listen to a single word.
"No voice! No choice!" the people cried,
"We want to be free!" they said with pride.

So brave leaders gathered from every land,
To write a letter, bold and grand.
They met in summer, in a room so hot,
To write down their thoughts, a very big plot!

9

A clever man named Thomas Jefferson
Picked up his pen, and he got it done!
He wrote the words that we still say,
About freedom, rights, and a brand-new way.

"We believe," the letter said, loud and clear,
"That all people are equal and dear.
We have the right to live and be free,
To chase our dreams and just be 'me'!"

13

This special paper told the king,
"We won't be ruled by your every word.
We want to choose our own new way,
So, we declare our freedom today!"

IN CONGRESS, JULY 4, 1776.

The unanimous Declaration · United States of America.

They called it the Declaration of Independence,
A name that shows strength and confidence.
It was signed on July Fourth, so true—
That's why we celebrate with red, white, and blue!

John Hancock signed his name so big and first,
Right in the middle and he was not coerced!
Others followed, bold and proud,
They signed that letter and read it aloud.

This document changed the world that day,

It helped start the United States in a brand-new way.

It said, "We are free! We will stand tall!

We'll make our own rules, once and for all!"

21

The Declaration still matters, even now,
It reminds us of freedom and keeping our vow.
That people have rights no one can take,
And fairness and justice are laws we make.

So, when you see fireworks lighting the sky,
Or you wave a flag as parades pass by,
Remember the agreement made so long ago,
By people who wanted the world to know—

"We believe in freedom, in being strong and kind,

In letting every person shine and speak their mind.

That's what the Declaration of Independence is really about!

So, let's thank God and give a shout!"

The End

The Declaration of Independence

In Congress, July 4, 1776

The unanimous Declaration of the thirteen united States of America, When in the Course of human events, it becomes necessary for one people to dissolve the political bands which have connected them with another, and to assume among the powers of the earth, the separate and equal station to which the Laws of Nature and of Nature's God entitle them, a decent respect to the opinions of mankind requires that they should declare the causes which impel them to the separation.

We hold these truths to be self-evident, that all men are created equal, that they are endowed by their Creator with certain unalienable Rights, that among these are Life, Liberty and the pursuit of Happiness.--That to secure these rights, Governments are instituted among Men, deriving their just powers from the consent of the governed, --That whenever any Form of Government becomes destructive of these ends, it is the Right of the People to alter or to abolish it, and to institute new Government, laying its foundation on such principles and organizing its powers in such form, as to them shall seem most likely to effect their Safety and

Happiness. Prudence, indeed, will dictate that Governments long established should not be changed for light and transient causes; and accordingly, all experience hath shown, that mankind is more disposed to suffer, while evils are sufferable, than to right themselves by abolishing the forms to which they are accustomed. But when a long train of abuses and usurpations, pursuing invariably the same Object evinces a design to reduce them under absolute Despotism, it is their right, it is their duty, to throw off such Government, and to provide new Guards for their future security.--Such has been the patient sufferance of these Colonies; and such is now the necessity which constrains them to alter their former Systems of Government. The history of the present King of Great Britain is a history of repeated injuries and usurpations, all having in direct object the establishment of an absolute Tyranny over these States. To prove this, let Facts be submitted to a candid world.

He has refused his Assent to Laws, the most wholesome and necessary for the public good.

He has forbidden his Governors to pass Laws of immediate and pressing importance, unless suspended in their operation till his Assent should be obtained; and when so suspended, he has utterly neglected to attend to them.

He has refused to pass other Laws for the accommodation of large districts of people, unless those people would relinquish the right of Representation in the Legislature, a right inestimable to them and formidable to tyrants only.

He has called together legislative bodies at places unusual, uncomfortable, and distant from the depository of their public Records, for the sole purpose of fatiguing them into compliance with his measures.

He has dissolved Representative Houses repeatedly, for opposing with manly firmness his invasions on the rights of the people.

He has refused for a long time, after such dissolutions, to cause others to be elected; whereby the Legislative powers, incapable of Annihilation, have returned to the People at large for their exercise; the State remaining in the meantime exposed to all the dangers of invasion from without, and convulsions within.

He has endeavored to prevent the population of these States; for that purpose, obstructing the Laws for Naturalization of Foreigners; refusing to pass others to encourage their migrations hither and raising the conditions of new Appropriations of Lands.

He has obstructed the Administration of Justice, by refusing his Assent to Laws for establishing Judiciary powers.

He has made Judges dependent on his Will alone, for the tenure of their offices, and the amount and payment of their salaries.

He has erected a multitude of New Offices and sent hither swarms of Officers to harass our people and eat out their substance.

He has kept among us, in times of peace, Standing Armies without the Consent of our legislatures.

He has affected to render the Military independent of and superior to the Civil power.

He has combined with others to subject us to a jurisdiction foreign to our constitution, and unacknowledged by our laws; giving his Assent to their Acts of pretended Legislation:

For Quartering large bodies of armed troops among us:

For protecting them, by a mock Trial, from punishment for any Murders which they should commit on the Inhabitants of these States:

For cutting off our Trade with all parts of the world:

For imposing Taxes on us without our Consent:

For depriving us in many cases, of the benefits of Trial by Jury:

For transporting us beyond Seas to be tried for pretended offences:

For abolishing the free System of English Laws in a neighboring Province, establishing therein an Arbitrary government, and enlarging its Boundaries so as to render it at once an example and fit instrument for introducing the same absolute rule into these Colonies:

For taking away our Charters, abolishing our most valuable Laws, and altering fundamentally the Forms of our Governments:

For suspending our own Legislatures and declaring themselves invested with power to legislate for us in all cases whatsoever.

He has abdicated Government here, by declaring us out of his Protection and waging War against us.

He has plundered our seas, ravaged our Coasts, burnt our towns, and destroyed the lives of our people.

He is at this time transporting large Armies of foreign Mercenaries to compleat the works of death, desolation and tyranny, already begun with circumstances of Cruelty & perfidy scarcely paralleled in the most barbarous ages, and totally unworthy the Head of a civilized nation.

He has constrained our fellow Citizens taken Captive on the high Seas to bear Arms against their Country, to become the executioners of their friends and Brethren, or to fall themselves by their Hands.

He has excited domestic insurrections amongst us and has endeavored to bring on the inhabitants of our frontiers, the merciless Indian Savages, whose known rule of warfare, is an undistinguished destruction of all ages, sexes and conditions.

In every stage of these Oppressions, We have Petitioned for Redress in the most humble terms: Our repeated Petitions have been answered only by repeated injury. A Prince, whose character is thus marked by every act which may define a Tyrant, is unfit to be the ruler of a free people.

Nor have We been wanting in attentions to our British brethren. We have warned them from time to time of attempts by their legislature to extend an unwarrantable jurisdiction over us. We have reminded them of the circumstances of our emigration and settlement here. We have appealed to their native justice and magnanimity, and we have conjured them by the ties of our common kindred to disavow these usurpations, which, would inevitably interrupt our connections and correspondence. They too have been deaf to the voice of justice and of consanguinity. We must, therefore, acquiesce in the necessity, which denounces our Separation, and hold them, as we hold the rest of mankind, Enemies in War, in Peace Friends.

We, therefore, the Representatives of the united States of America, in General Congress, Assembled, appealing to the Supreme Judge of the world for the rectitude of our intentions, do, in the Name, and by Authority of the good People of these Colonies, solemnly publish and declare, That these United Colonies are, and of Right ought to be Free and Independent States; that they are Absolved from all Allegiance to the British Crown, and that all political connection between them and the State of Great Britain, is and ought to be totally dissolved; and that as Free and Independent States, they have full Power to levy War, conclude Peace, contract Alliances, establish Commerce, and to do all other Acts and Things which Independent States may of right do. And for the support of this Declaration, with a firm reliance on the protection of divine Providence, we mutually pledge to each other our Lives, our Fortunes and our sacred Honor.

Signatures:

Georgia

Button Gwinnett

Lyman Hall

George Walton

North Carolina

William Hooper

Joseph Hewes

John Penn

South Carolina

Edward Rutledge

Thomas Heyward, Jr.

Thomas Lynch, Jr.

Arthur Middleton

Massachusetts

John Hancock

Maryland

Samuel Chase

William Paca

Thomas Stone

Charles Carroll of Carrollton

Virginia

George Wythe

Richard Henry Lee

Thomas Jefferson

Benjamin Harrison

Thomas Nelson, Jr.

Francis Lightfoot Lee

Carter Braxton

Pennsylvania

Robert Morris

Benjamin Rush

Benjamin Franklin

John Morton

George Clymer

James Smith

George Taylor

James Wilson

George Ross

Delaware

Caesar Rodney

George Read

Thomas McKean

New York

William Floyd

Philip Livingston

Francis Lewis

Lewis Morris

New Jersey

Richard Stockton

John Witherspoon

Francis Hopkinson

John Hart

Abraham Clark

New Hampshire

Josiah Bartlett

William Whipple

Massachusetts

Samuel Adams

John Adams

Robert Treat Paine

Elbridge Gerry

Rhode Island

Stephen Hopkins

William Ellery

Connecticut

Roger Sherman

Samuel Huntington

William Williams

Oliver Wolcott

New Hampshire

Matthew Thornton

www.ingramcontent.com/pod-product-compliance
Lightning Source LLC
Chambersburg PA
CBHW081541120626
46550CB00009B/2817

9781966491163